Praise for Body Wisdom

"Talia writes from the pain of her own personal journey with reflection and self-courage, which gives her writing a real depth and authenticity. There is an essential message of the need to listen to our own self and our body and to work with inner choice. As Talia states, the choice as to which 'wolf' we feed – I really loved that. Current trauma therapy is continually moving to the importance of body awareness and that the body also holds deep memory. Talia's own experience shows this power of the body to heal emotionally. So often it is from sharing the healing of personal traumas that others can also gain courage, so thank you Talia."

Dr Sue Lutton, Psychiatrist/Psychotherapist

"Talia's descriptions of the experience of perfectionism, anxiety, an eating disorder and depression were profoundly moving and gives the reader a poignant insight into those experiences. Her honesty shines through, like she is done hiding and there is nowhere else to go but the honest and raw experience. What also struck me is her bravery in sharing those incredibly painful experiences. I loved the poetry at the beginning of the chapters."

Terry Levingthal, Clinical Psychologist

"A truly positive reflection into understanding who we are and how our own choices feed our inner 'wolf'. Talia's journey shows us the damage caused by striving for those impossible 'perfectionistic' expectations. Yet throughout it all, she maintains an attitude of gratitude, acceptance and dedication to growth. She gently illustrates to the reader the importance of taking self-responsibility, and that it is only "I" who can heal my life, no one else, whilst simultaneously reminding us that in our interconnectedness we are never alone."

Miriam Munitz, Human Resources

"Talia's background in traditional medicine, combined with her understanding of the spiritual and esoteric, can help forge that bridge that needs so desperately to be laid for the world. To combine science and spirituality is like the merging of the divine masculine and divine feminine in each of us – something the world desperately needs in all areas."

Elaine Macleod, Reiki Practitioner

Body Wisdom

Body Wisdom
What is Your Body Trying to Tell You?

Dr Talia Steed

Copyright © 2022 Dr Talia Steed

All rights reserved. Without limiting the rights under copyright reserved, no part of this publication may be reproduced, stored or introduced into a retrieval system, or transmitted in any form or by any means (electronic, mechanical, photocopying, recording or otherwise) without the prior written permission of both the copyright owners and the publisher of this book. The author does not provide medical advice or prescribe the use of any technique as a form of treatment for mental health or medical problems without the advice of a physician. The intent of the author is only to offer information to help you in your quest for emotional wellbeing. In the event you use any of the information in this book for yourself, the author and the publisher assume no responsibility. The names of the participants in the stories are altered to respect their privacy.

A catalogue record for this book is available from the National Library of Australia

ISBN: 978-0-6454165-0-3 (print)
ISBN: 978-0-6454165-1-0 (epub)

Interior and Cover Design: Pickawoowoo Publishing Group
Print and Distribution Ingram (AUS / US/ UK /EUR)

Body Wisdom

What is Your Body Trying to Tell You?

Body wisdom teaches us how to tune into the wisdom of the body, to reach an optimal state of health, wellness, peace and contentment.

It is the practice of bypassing the chatter of the active human mind to receive guidance from within.

Through learning to listen to the signals of our body we can connect more deeply with our true self, beyond the external influences of the world.

Dr Talia Steed

Contents

Foreword xi

One	The Story of Me	1
Two	Perfectionism	7
Three	The Eating Disordered Brain	15
Four	Depression	27
Five	Faith	41
Six	Listening to My Body	45
Seven	Body Wisdom	55
Eight	How to Listen to our Body	62
Nine	The Path to Healing	66
Ten	Messages from within our own body	69

About the Author 73
Acknowledgments 75
Final Dedication 77

Foreword

Dr Ahmed Munib
MBBS, Mphil (Psychiatry), PhD (UniMelb), FRANZCP|
Consultant Psychiatrist/Clinical Associate Professor (UWA)

The book *Body Wisdom* that you hold in your hands is more than a collection of words, sentences and ideas. It is the tangible essence and inspirational self-portrait of the author, Dr Talia Steed, and the conglomeration of the many challenges and obstacles she has encountered and prevailed through during her professional and personal journey in life.

However, for us – the reader – to fully appreciate and acknowledge this unique and intimate book, we must attempt to comprehend the author and the person behind *Body Wisdom*.

My very first encounter with Talia was approximately a decade prior in a public metropolitan hospital mental health outpatient clinic. It was a bright summer morning and I had been informed that a new doctor had reported for duty on her first day in the department. Talia had been assigned as a trainee registrar with the Royal Australian and New Zealand College of Psychiatrists (RANZCP), as part of her scheduled six months rotation. I was the allocated supervisor for the term rotation, and unequivocally aware of the extremely competitive nature of being selected as a registrar with the highly prestigious RANZCP training program.

At the initial impression, Talia expressed herself as a demure, soft-spoken and highly intelligent young doctor, with only a few years of recency from medical school graduation. I would continue to work with and supervise Talia over the duration of her clinical rotation in psychiatry, becoming promptly familiar with Talia's unique abilities to connect with complex mental health patients, and meaningfully extrapolate their stories. She exhibited an innate ability to explore mental illness processes and psychopathologies with great compassion, profound empathy and circumspect commitment. Talia was exceptionally conscientious with resolute professionalism, demonstrating an in-depth maturity and introspection far beyond that usually observed in a young person in their late 20s. There was a consistently vibrant and effervescent aura of intellectual curiosity as Talia delicately navigated the meandering trajectory of the training program curriculum.

Talia successfully completed her six-month rotation, unsurprisingly scoring at the 'surpasses the expected standard' level. However, she left an indelible impression on her multidisciplinary work colleagues – junior and senior doctors, mental health nurses, social workers and allied health workers, to cite only a few. Even many months after completion of her training placement, others in the workplace would inquire about Talia and positively comment on her diligence, kindness, sense of responsibility and quiet dignity.

Over the past decade, Talia has explored various professional avenues, and even where there have been barriers and obstacles, she has created her very own doors and stepped confidently along new pathways. I have been privileged to maintain a somewhat remote mentoring role for Talia, offering guidance and advice when needed and requested. It has indeed been fulfilling to observe and appreciate Talia's resilience and fortitude in overcoming significant physical and mental health challenges, to become the person she is today.

Body Wisdom has been created in the crucible of Talia's compelling and extraordinary journey of self-reflection and discovery. Reading her erudite and eloquent story may bring you closer to understanding your own self, and perhaps enlighten and reward you with the gift of knowing a genuinely remarkable and altruistic individual.

One

The Story of Me

Throughout my personal healing journey and my professional life as a doctor, I was repeatedly faced with the limitations of modern medicine. There were no answers to be found for my symptoms from within the medical model and so this prompted my search for other options. However, what I found was that despite what modality I tried, I could not seem to find the solutions.

At the same time, I was seeing patients going through the exact same situation. Faced with these limitations, I knew there must be something more. Body wisdom is the meeting point between science and psyche. It encompasses all modalities as tools that are chosen depending on what our body tells us we need.

This is where lies the art. As we learn to tune in to our inner wisdom, we can uncover the exact modality, food, behaviour or change we need to make to take that first stepping stone on the path to health.

The conscious mind is only a small part of the human psyche. The subconscious beliefs we carry make up a much greater part of what dictates our behaviours, often, as in the case of ill-health, keeping us stuck. Body wisdom helps us access the subconscious insights we carry.

It works because there is no single-fit approach to healing as we are each such unique individuals with layers of complexity. Our answers lie within. With the space and stillness to uncover what these are, we can create our own healing path.

My journey as a highly sensitive female doctor in a modern Western society, has taken me down a unique path of exploring the concept of healing. I have come to deeply appreciate and understand the way in which our body is constantly trying to communicate with us. Many patients present to the doctor every day with troubling physical symptoms that they want quickly alleviated. We have been conditioned to believe that a symptom is something to be treated and forgotten, so we can just get on with our busy lives. It is becoming more widely recognised though, that there is a link between the physical symptoms we experience and the mental, emotional and psychological aspects of our lives.

Body Wisdom

My journey through physical and mental health issues has shown me that there is no coincidence in the symptoms we experience. I have learnt that when I really tune in to my body's inner wisdom, I can connect with my truth instead of letting the mind dictate. Our thoughts, emotions and sensations can be fleeting and temporary, but the body shows us what we need to know. If we choose to listen.

My hope is that my story will shed the light on what happens when we go against the wisdom of the body and how at any moment we have the choice to pay attention and heal. I have found that when we ask the question, "What is your body trying to tell you?" from a calm and centred place, we can delve deeper into this inner guidance system and get the answers we need from deep within. Too often we go searching for our answers in the outside world, only to develop even more confusion. When we instead come back to ourselves and our body in the present moment, we can access the truth of what we need and embark on our own daring adventure.

I came into this world as a highly sensitive person. This has shaped my life both positively and negatively. Without this trait I would not know the world in its depth, in its subtleties and in its colour. Being a highly sensitive person means that I can feel everything very intensely. This has given me some of the positive qualities that I am grateful constitute who I am as a person. I am a highly empathic friend, confidante and healer. Since childhood I have had an innate ability to step into others shoes on a deeper level than simply understanding their perspective, and feeling into the core of their position. But with these attributes comes the more difficult and at times painful and distressing side of this trait. I have also felt for most of my life, the depth and extremes of the negative emotional states available to us as human beings. Hence the journey towards equanimity has been a focus point in my life.

Faced with a world in which being highly sensitive is a minority trait and where society places value on being extraverted, social, entertaining and fast-paced, we as the highly sensitive enter the world being different. Trying to mould myself to fit in with these pressures and expectations resulted in being faced with the effects of an overwhelmed, highly sensitive person.

My parents were emigrants from South Africa, a country that was rooted in fear. Our ancestors were Jewish, a people who were always afraid of being persecuted. As an infant of less than a year old I was flown across the world to this new, blissful land of Australia, to be gifted with the upbringing of a safe, peaceful city. Some may think on surface appearances that how could such a small child know of the fear she had been exposed to, from that which she had emerged. Yet it was in my blood, coursing through every cell in my body. Fear was my DNA.

As the sensitive sponge that I was in my early years, I was surrounded by the energy of two parents who had left all they knew to allow their children the privilege of a safe and secure upbringing. Call it genes, add on environment, multiply by the highly sensitive trait, female sex, first born and you have one very scared, fearful being at her core.

In the early years I don't recall feeling scared or anxious as such, but I was definitely emotional, strong willed and a fiery spirit! My mother, coming from a generation that knew far less about emotional regulation than we know today, was faced with the challenge of parenting someone so similar. At eighteen months she took me to see a professional for my 'difficult behaviour', who told her there was nothing wrong with her child. Yet due to the highly impressionable mind we have as children, I internalised the belief, like so many of us do for a variety of different reasons, that there was something inherently wrong with me.

The overlap here between being highly sensitive and anxious in my opinion is huge. Being highly sensitive means that you are going to be anxious in the outside world when you are trying so hard not to upset anyone and be what is expected of you. This makes home relationships difficult though and the combination of an anxious parent with an anxious child can lead to a very overwhelmed and heightened emotional home environment.

If we can educate parents to understand their child's unique make up, they can be better equipped to handle and support their child. This can shift the whole trajectory of a child's life to becoming someone who can emotionally regulate and develop enough self-support to get through the challenges and obstacles of life.

Pearls of Wisdom:

- You are not your story.
- At any moment we have the capability to say, "This is not where my journey will end."
- The point of power lies in taking self-responsibility and ownership over the circumstances we have created in our lives.
- It is up to each one of us to recreate our life from the inside out, and create the version of our life we wish to live.

Two

Perfectionism

As I continued my journey I came to discover that a way of making everyone happy and receiving praise and esteem was from doing well at school, just as many children are conditioned to believe. From an early age I was classified as a 'diligent hard worker', who was organised, well behaved and the 'perfect' student. I thrived in this role. I loved my teachers, was content with my friends and overall lived a happy uneventful childhood. There was much joy and laughter growing up, with the ocean, creativity, swimming and play shaping most of my childhood memories.

When I shifted to high school I was well aware of not liking to be the centre of attention and would shut down when in large groups, fearful to speak up, but that was the only thing I remember about having any significant fears. As

I progressed through high school my identity as the diligent student only intensified, as I became determined and preoccupied with the idea of becoming a doctor. I think part of it was to show my mother that I could. Growing up with two highly intelligent brothers, my small ego self felt I was not considered as intelligent. I also knew in my heart I wanted to make a difference to the lives of others, and in my childhood naivety and conditioned belief systems, this was the best way to go about doing it. However, I loved my school days, the structure, the routine and the predictability of it were all elements that appealed to my rigid personality at that time. I also gained a strong sense of self through achieving. When I worked hard and then was rewarded with good grades, I felt validated, good about myself – as if I could accomplish anything.

The stress of being perfect in this domain of life started to cause me significant anxiety and distress though, as I obsessively pursued this path. In Year 12 this manifested as heightened levels of stress, with episodes of crying and becoming overwhelmed in the year co-ordinator's office. I continued to study extremely hard, in my mind in an attempt to achieve my full academic potential. I had rigid schedules every day of homework, assignments and studying for tests, and when exams came around these were intensified. I made sure to never let a single question go by that I didn't understand the answer to. This meant that lunch times and often after school were spent with teachers, making sure I was 100 per cent prepared for each assessment, to give myself the best possible chance of reaching that 100 per cent grade. I don't recall having physical symptoms of anxiety at that stage, but back then I didn't even know what the meaning of the word was. I was obsessively focused on my academic performance and getting into Medicine at UWA, at the expense of anything and everything else.

The structured routine of school kept things contained though, as life remained in relative control. It wasn't until leaving school and embarking upon the outside world of uncertainty, unpredictability and to my small self, chaos, that the path took on an uphill battle of challenges to overcome.

At the time and for many years after, I strongly held the belief that there were no external pressures placed upon me. I believed the extreme levels of stress and worry I had experienced related to academic performance, were purely a result of my inner pressures, perfectionism and the desire to achieve. However, with time I have reflected on the impact of our cultural conditioning linking achievement with academic success, as a significant external pressure. There was definitely some emphasis placed on being a caring and kind person and being of service in the world. However, the two important concepts of intuition and emotional regulation were not prioritised. With an intuitive compass young people would be better placed to identify the best direction they would be suited to take after leaving high school. Also, educating children with tools to assist in managing emotions and learning to self-support would result in more resilient adults able to navigate the pressures and demands of our very fast paced modern world.

I read a quote once that said, "Striving for excellence is motivating, but striving for perfection is demoralising." This is an understatement, but is true in its simplicity. Perfectionism is beyond demoralising. It can be soul destroying. Rationally we all know that it doesn't really exist, yet when this is our make-up we innately strive to reach it, especially when we are not conscious and discerning of our actions. Perfectionism has infiltrated my life in multiple domains. Firstly, my academic drive went far beyond simply trying 'to do well at school' and 'get good grades'. This intensity of effort was unsustainable and so following Year 12 I found myself unable to continue to put in as much work, even throughout medical school. I had already burnt myself out.

Other areas of my life that the perfectionistic trait has seeped into over the years are relationships, daily life, hobbies, anything really. This places enormous pressure on just being in the world. A life of endless 'shoulds' is exhausting. "I should do this" or, "We should be like that". All sense of joy, ease and lightness to life is removed by the desire to reach the unattainable. I often wondered why every day of my life for many years seemed like such a struggle. Beyond the tangible difficulties I encountered in the outside world, simply existing was an effort.

I have since learnt the damaging and violent nature of the word 'should'. In yoga there is a concept called *ahimsa*, or non-violence. A teacher of mine many times emphasised to us in class that 'should' is one of these violent words. Life is restricted when we are confined by the constructs of how we think we 'should' act, or do what we think we 'should' do. It hinders creativity, vitality and our passion and thirst for life. What I have come to learn is that life is not about endless pain and the creation of suffering, but about seeking joy and finding the blessings amongst the challenges and obstacles that every human life encounters. This is what it means to live a truly graceful and contented life. Not having everything go exactly right or be how you think it 'should' be, but maintaining an attitude of peace and contentment regardless of what external circumstances you face. This is by no means an easy task, to repeatedly choose love and step away from our fear-based conditioned responses, but the benefits to our entire being are always worth it.

Perfectionism also stops you from doing things, because if you know you can't do something that meets the standard you desire, you just don't do it. This is one of the reasons I struggled with medicine. It would be impossible for anyone to obtain all the knowledge in the field. Or any field for that matter, but being a junior doctor requires such a broad knowledge base. And starting such a degree, as a burnt out Year 12 with undetected anxiety seeking perfection, was the 'perfect' combination for what was to come in my life.

For the first thirty years of my life I was also very much someone who internalised everything and believed if things didn't go right they were somehow my fault. Yet what I have come to learn is just how much the interplay of external factors with our internal traits contributes to the formation of our belief systems. No one is immune from the dynamics and influences of family, community, city, country and the world at large. We are all products of it. We are all subject to absorbing the dominant belief structures that surround us, especially those of us who are more sensitive.

Within my family I recall feeling like the odd one out. There were my two parents, my two brothers, and then me. As a child I was in constant power struggles with my mother. We would be extremely close one moment and completely raging against each other the next – the story of many mother-daughter relationships. My father stepped back from this dynamic, present in the physical sense but less so emotionally. I found that our difficulty in navigating conflict contributed to me developing patterns of trying to please others to avoid unmanageable emotional reactions and I became fearful of making others angry.

As time went on I attracted relationships and situations that perpetuated this dynamic, with the submissive aspect of my personality becoming progressively more pronounced. My inner fire was being extinguished by these subsequent experiences in the medical field and intimate relationships. I found that my emotions were seen negatively by others and myself, as no one seemed to know how to deal with them, least of all me. On some level I held the belief there was something fundamentally wrong with who I was.

These dynamics by no means detracted from the unconditional love and care I received and still do to this day. I feel so blessed to have been gifted these two souls as my parents, to walk with on this journey in this lifetime. As I have shifted and evolved over the years, so have they. Whenever I needed someone to vent to, I was met with the safety and love of my mother's ears. She listened to it all. Supporting me in every way she knew how. My father and I have also developed a strong bond founded on mutual respect and understanding. He has supported me emotionally and practically through challenging circumstances, and I am so grateful that we have been gifted the opportunities to transform our relationship. Without the gift of these two souls I don't know how I would have endured the karmic lessons my soul needed to heal.

As a family we have facilitated much soul growth in one another as we navigate our way through the dynamics and complexities of family relationships. The beauty of mine is that there is a deep, enduring and unconditional love between us. I have come to appreciate the importance of allowing others to be who they are, rather than who you want them to be. Through cultivating more acceptance and less judgement towards others, they become freer to share their love and truth with you. This is the path towards true connection, when each person can simply be who they are, without feeling the need to modify themselves to present the aspect they believe is what other people want to see.

Pearls of Wisdom:

- Perfectionism is an illusion.
- In yogic philosophy the idea is that we put in our best efforts and surrender the results.
- And best efforts will vary depending on what else is going on for us.
- We are human beings and we will make mistakes, wrong decisions and fail. But this itself is perfect in teaching us the lessons we are meant to learn and allowing us to have a rich and meaningful human experience of life.

Three

The Eating Disordered Brain

The impact of perfectionism in my life also contributed to the development of an eating disorder. It was almost as if once the drive and focus on school was removed, my perfectionistic brain needed a new target. That target became my body. I started out as many young girls do, wanting to 'lose a few kilos' and 'tone up'. Conditioned by the external world to believe that we are not enough and not okay as we are. However, this spiralled into obsessively monitoring everything I consumed. It shifted beyond wanting to look attractive or desirable to the opposite sex – a young and insecure attitude – to an obsessive pursuit of my irrational version of perfection.

To continue my journey through my twenties I was faced with many uphill battles, that constitute the hero's journey that is all of our lives. To think that it is only us who suffer is an illusion, "Maya". But often our small ego self likes to convince us that this is so. As human beings we all suffer, but we also all have the capacity to transcend suffering when we awaken to the truth of our being, our higher self, which is who we really are.

The anxiety that I experienced throughout my twenties further perpetuated the very extreme fears of food that took hold of my being. The preoccupation was linked to control, when everything else seemed so fragile and uncertain. If I could somehow control what I put into my body and my weight itself, in some irrational way things could be more manageable. So along with a lack of power, inner trust and self-belief that held my being captive to the story of struggle, the fear of eating meant every time I was to consume something my system would go into a stress response. Danger. Shut down. The brain perceives this emotional threat in the same way as it does a physical threat to our safety, which also contributed to the cultivation of years of gastrointestinal disease.

Round and round you go, like a record on repeat.
Clinging to something to create some sense of security, stability, safety when inside I feel lost, unsettled, uncertain and afraid.
Round and round you go, on the merry go round of thought.
Distraction, distraction. Why do you trouble me so?
Can't I have some rest, some reprieve?
Quiet. Please? STOP! I beg and pray.
Take these thoughts out of my brain.

Let me have some peace and stillness.
Round and round, the record on repeat.
Louder, softer, LOUDER. TOO loud.
Panic.
Stress.
Take them away! A moment's peace.
That's what I crave.
Please! Please!
Make them go away.

For a long time I had to work at rewiring my brain to accept that food was not a threat. That instead it is there to nurture and nourish my body, my being, so I can function optimally in the world and do what I have come to this earth to do – to fulfil my dharma, my life's path, my destiny. I have had to re-evaluate every routine behaviour and thought through the cultivation of the witness-observer mind. I have had to stop and assess whether each action, thought and belief is actually serving me. What this process has shown me is that often we are doing things that are only perpetuating the issue, until we can cultivate enough self-awareness to illuminate what is not serving us.

Although over all the years I maintained a sufficient balance of intake and exercise such that I was never unwell enough to require any form of acute intervention – and I never skipped a meal, binged or purged – I still had what I describe as the "anorexic brain" within my head. With so many restrictive rules and limitations, it was a daily battle I would face with my mind, never free from thinking about food. Now I can comprehend the gravity of the anxiety that accompanied these thoughts. I was constantly on edge about either what I had eaten or a meal to come. The joy was removed from most social occasions, as I was so preoccupied with my internal distress.

Over the years I journaled about it when I either thought I was willing to do something to change things, or when it was overcoming me to such an extent that I had to express it. However, the rest of the time I lived in denial. When those around me would try to raise their concerns, I would become extremely anxious and very defensive. It's scary how powerful this disorder can become. For instance, I held an entrenched belief that the people who most love me in this world were somehow trying to trick me by telling me I was too thin or needed to look at my diet. For a long time this was the hardest aspect of myself to share. It felt like a secret, ironically, though was obvious to the outside world manifesting in changes to my physical body. Another trick of the disorder – locking you into your own mind and prison.

An eating disorder is a powerful thing. Let loose it can destruct the spirit and change the course of a life. For me it probably began as a child. Well the beginnings of something that had the potential to get out of control. Already in primary school I was aware of food and what I consumed. I remember on occasions writing down what I wanted to eat and how much I wanted to exercise and when I did not meet my expectations I was disappointed and judgemental of my behaviour. At the time it did not consume my life or thoughts throughout the day. However, it was something that was in my consciousness and sidelined for wanting to excel at school, develop friendships and enjoy my childhood.

When I was in high school I was aware of my body and how it made me feel, but I was so focused on achieving that although issues about weight and food got me down they were not the primary focus of my life. It was just before my eighteenth birthday when I was looking for something to wear and nothing seemed to look right, when something clicked in my head that set me down the path that was to dominate my thoughts and life for so long.

I think, looking back on it all now, there were also other factors that contributed to the development of the eating disorder, one of them being the intensity of the medical degree and my ambivalence about choosing the right career path. After being at the top of the class in year eleven and twelve, I was now faced with being one of many intelligent students who I felt were more "naturally smart" than myself. I constantly feared being unable to obtain the knowledge required to become a good doctor. I guess it made me feel out of control, and the one thing I still could completely control was what I put into my body and how I looked on the outside.

The impact of anxiety is very closely linked with the development of eating disorders, as well as the perfectionist personality type.

With an eating disorder, there are so many contributing factors that just kind of fall into place and all of a sudden it is something that almost defines who you are. And the difficult thing is to break this pattern. But as everyone is well aware of, the worst of habits are the hardest to break. Eating disorders are all about rigidity, in eating patterns and exercise routines. Challenging this structured way of behaving can feel impossible to even attempt.

The wider impact on friends and family is also something that often the sufferer is ignorant of. When I developed more insight I felt sad for the worry and stress experienced by my mother in particular. Imagine seeing your one and only daughter go through something so self-destructive at a time in her life that could be so enjoyable. Especially during the times that I went to her crying, revealing how much judgement, extreme criticism and disapproval I was directing towards myself. I knew rationally that I needed to see myself in the same light as I see all others, and allow myself the same flexibility to be human and make human mistakes as everyone else. However, taking action on this was a significant obstacle to be overcome.

Another aspect of the illness is when the mind starts to become obsessed with thoughts about food when the body is deprived of it. It makes sense really that if some things are considered the wrong types of food to consume, the mind is constantly thinking about ways to avoid situations in which it would be confronted with these foods. This makes life a lot harder because certain restaurants where I wouldn't want to eat are often places that other people choose to have group dinners. So, then thoughts arise in my mind not only related to food, but also revolving around the anxiety of how I am going to handle the situation.

Another situation that is very difficult is going to people's houses for dinner, especially when you don't know the people very well. These are the things someone with an eating disorder *faces — anxiety and worry about normal everyday experiences that are often considered relaxing and enjoyable for other people. And the result is often isolation. When you are so focused on the meal and what people might be thinking about your response to it, you can often become quiet and uninvolved in the conversation. This only functions to bring a sense of shame and embarrassment about the peculiarities of your behaviour and your difference to others.*

The physical effects of food deprivation and restriction are significant on the thought processes of the mind. It may not be as extreme for me as deprivation because I never once starved myself and probably have never missed a meal in my life. However, when the body is deprived of variety you become deficient in certain essential vitamins and minerals. A balanced diet provides the brain with the energy and variety it needs to function at its optimum and focus its attention on the task at hand, rather than being distracted by useless thoughts about food, noise that prevents you from seeing what's really in front of you.

The distraction is unbearable. Living in the present moment becomes such a transient state of existence as you seem to always be fluctuating between past and future events. However, it is very hard to change your thoughts once they have been a certain way for a long time and so the process is a very slow, ambivalent one.

Another sad reality of the eating disorder is the rigidity I felt about sticking to certain meal times in order to avoid feeling extremely depleted of energy. As I would only want to eat a certain amount of food a day, I would sometimes hold off until dinner instead of having too many snacks, which would leave me feeling very weak and hungry. So, of course thoughts would revolve around food — how could they not when our primary instinct as animals is to obtain enough food and water to survive? The mind of someone with an eating disorder becomes her enemy, and sometimes you feel like you just want to escape from the pressures it is placing on how you live your life.

Despite having friends, a boyfriend and a good family, the isolation that accompanies an eating disorder is something that is also hard to live with. At times you just feel so alone and that no one understands what you are going through. There's no one to talk to and life just feels like a routine that needs to be kept in check. I have felt at numerous points that there's no point in continuing in such a depressing state of existence, yet this still didn't prompt me to change my behaviour. It's a feeling of being so trapped within your own head and thoughts and wanting so desperately for things to be different, but at the same time so intensely feeling the fear of gaining too much weight. Also, you feel that you don't want anyone to know the reality of what is going on inside your head in fear of being told that things have to change.

It is a constant challenge at the moment as I continue to change my dietary behaviours, not to focus on what I've eaten, but I know that the most important thing is to keep pushing at the resistance within my mind to these changes. Instead I know I should focus on the future where these behaviours will be accepted within my own mind as the norm. It is harder to do though and I just have hope that over time it will become easier.

With the passing of time…

One of the things that came up from when I was in a different place in the past was the anxiety I felt when people would comment on my looking well. Innocent comments that people used to make that were intended to make me feel good about myself caused intense anxiety for me. I felt that if they were commenting on how 'nice' I was looking it meant that I had obviously put on a noticeable amount of weight, which I saw as such a negative thing. Now I have the insight to acknowledge that it was a positive change that they were observing in me, as I went from looking unnaturally thin to more feminine.

Something else that came up was my intense desire to be able to fit into clothes that I had worn at my thinnest. In the same way as other people's comments affected me, I felt that this was such a negative thing when I was unable to do so. Also on reflection, these issues consumed me to such an extent that they were the most central aspect of my life. So, when clothes were tighter than they had been, this was devastating to me and took over my entire inner world. The more I express these thoughts though, the more I can see the irrationality behind them. It's so incredibly difficult for circumstances to change when a person is still in such a state of denial, both to others and herself. I feel that it is only now that I have come to truly accept and express the reality of my experiences, that I can really move forward.

And I have noticed within myself how much more enjoyable life is when I am not preoccupied with other thoughts. I have had enough of being trapped within my own head and have taken the initial steps towards a life free from this illness. I was once told that the average time span of an eating disorder is five years. I am now twenty-two going on twenty-three. I have done my time.

3 years on...

I have just skimmed through what I have written previously and it makes me sad to think and say that I am still consumed by these thoughts. The positives are that I have gained weight and am in the process of accepting it. I wouldn't say that I 100 per cent accept the weight gain, but I know that it was necessary as I wasn't having regular periods and I was still quite selective in what I would eat. I want to have a normal relationship with food, but this has affected my thought processes.

I still repeat in my mind what I have eaten, like a broken record replaying the same meaningless sentences over and over again. I know they're only thoughts, however they are distressing for me when I feel as if I can't or won't stop them. So where do I go from here? What would I say to my own patient going through this? Well, I would reassure her that she was in a positive place and that she had made huge progress. I would remind her of what she has, a loving and supportive family, some really close girlfriends, a good career ahead of her and the insight to understand and help her own patients. I would encourage her to be mindful of old thought processes and label them as 'those old eating thoughts'. To create more periods of silence in her world and give her mind the chance to experience some moments of clarity and stillness. To accept her illness, herself – her whole self, both body and mind. And remind her that she is lucky to be getting there, and that it is always two steps forward one step back, until you are completely rid of old bad habits.

Rereading my writings from, firstly, twenty-two and then around twenty-five, has been confronting to see how much I had been suffering all those years. Now I am twenty-nine, another four years has passed on. In that time I definitely became more restrictive and lost weight, probably to a point either the same or worse than I had been in the earlier years. This was a result of other stressful life experiences that contributed to me clinging to this way of artificially creating a sense of control, in what felt like a totally chaotic and unpredictable existence.

Where I am at now is finally accepting, for a much more prolonged period without denial, the significance and gravity of this disorder on my life. I have had multiple realisations of late that my behaviour had completely spiralled out of control. It was controlling me. It has been scary to face these realisations, especially when I have looked at parts of my body as if I am seeing them for the first time. My perception was so distorted that I didn't grasp how I actually looked to others, as when I look in the mirror I mostly get tricked by my mind into believing I just look slim and how I 'should' be. An eating disordered brain is like a battlefield with the most harsh, extreme opponent imaginable. And I am honestly just beginning to enter into the fight, but I have seen glimpses of a new life in every small change I make and thought I challenge.

My aim in sharing some of these most private and personal thoughts and experiences along the journey, is to provide a true, in-depth insight into some of the realities of living with an eating disorder. I want to show how when it truly sets in, an eating disorder goes so much further beyond the physical body and outside appearance, as it creates the most immense turmoil, conflict, suffering and entrapment of the thought processes in the mind of the sufferer. And the distortion of the mind is unimaginable.

Looking back on this I can see that the implications of being in a dysfunctional relationship in which I was condemned for being who I was as an Empath, in conjunction with being in the medical profession which held the same attitude, were two major perpetuating factors for my prolonged battle. However, to take ownership of my role in these dynamics, means to acknowledge that I allowed this. I allowed others to treat me with such disregard and disrespect, because I did not love the person I was. I had no connection to my true self and was lost within the pressures and expectations of the external world.

Pearls of Wisdom:

- We are so much more than the physical bodies we inhabit.
- Our body is simply the shell or vehicle through which our soul can move through the journey of life.
- When we love and respect ourself we treat our body in the most loving, kindest ways.
- Listening to the needs of our body is one of the greatest lessons we learn as human beings. When we go against what the body needs we experience ill health. Healing is the path to self-love and acceptance.

Four

Depression

As I continued on my journey following the end of high school, with my belief structures and limited views of the world in place, I ventured off into the world of university. Medical school. For an Empath, highly sensitive soul and female this equated to a living nightmare! Sadly, the conditioned patriarchal culture of Western society – the epitome of this being the foundations of the 'old-school' medical belief system – meant that I found myself within an environment that was toxic and damaging to my psyche and spirit.

Enough's enough
They cannot understand.
They do not see.
I know I am different. I do not see the world like they do.

They exist on a level of life that is foreign to me.
Yet I will no longer let them take my power.
I will not cry and fall apart, trying so hard to mould myself to be who I am not.
That is not the path of the higher truth of my being, or yours.
I will not shrink to make myself small, keeping them strong by fuelling their flame with the light of my own.

Enough's enough.
But I will become smarter.
I will learn the game I have to play.
Not with fear, or negativity, or resistance, or anger.
I will play in the name of love.
In the name of truth.
I will follow my path for the sake of the greater good of the evolution of our collective consciousness.

I will not give up.
I will be the light worker that I agreed to be.
The choice is mine.
The choice is yours.
The choice is all of ours to make.
Fear or love.
Shrink or sore.
I will have faith.
Trust.
Knowing I am exactly where I am meant to be.
No more tears.

Shedding victim self.
Power.
Power versus force.
True power.
Inner strength.
I will not give up!

At the same time I found myself in a long-term relationship that similarly was based on the belief structure that emotions and sensitivity were somehow inferior. This was simply the result of choosing the wrong partner, yet paradoxically the exact partner I needed to catapult me down a path of spiritual awakening and expansion. A person so enmeshed in the conditioned tribal notion of what it means to be a 'strong' person that any emotional expression or deviating from 'what we do' or 'what is done' was condoned. This is by no means a blame on who he is or was, as he, like us all, is simply a product of our environmental and cultural conditioning, until we cultivate enough awareness to conduct a new way of being in the world. If we choose to.

Broken. Shattered. Heart bleeding open on the floor.
How will I ever repair my wounded heart?
Pain…literally in the centre of my chest.
How can an emotion cause such a deep ache into the inner most layers of my being?
How will I ever love again when love has felt so painful?
Mistrust.

Falling, falling.
Nothing safe.
No stable ground. Like the ground has fallen away from beneath my shell of a body.
Run…Run!
I must escape from these excruciating feelings.
Bubble wrap my heart.
No. Lock away my heart.
Iron steel gates…keep away the chance of this ever happening again.
Fearlessly independent.
That is what I shall become.
No one will hurt me like this again…

He broke my spirit.
He took away my sense of self-worth.
He looked at me like I was diseased.
Or not at all.
He worried that having a child with me would result in a child like me. So why did he say he loved me?
It broke my heart.
And I didn't love myself so allowed him to treat me like crap.
The looks, the disgust on his face.
Then saying I love you.
No wonder I was so confused.
My power was lost.
He said I wanted the best of both worlds, wouldn't work full time and wouldn't do all the household chores.
Yet I was breaking inside.

They told me I was incompetent.
Too emotional to be a real doctor.
Too anxious, too soft.
They cornered and bullied. And I allowed it.
I let them all treat me like nothing. No-thing.
I had no idea of my own self-worth.
I could not see that I was beautiful, strong, determined, loving, passionate, caring, compassionate, hard-working, loyal, trustworthy, gentle, forgiving, open-hearted, seeing the best in people, always.
I had no clue of my own self-worth.
My intelligence, capabilities, creativity.
I was blind. I was lost.
And every message I had ever heard was "You are not enough".
Not strong enough, not capable or competent enough, not assertive enough. Or too emotive, too anxious.
I just wanted them all to be happy.
But that was not my job.
I am only responsible for my own happiness. And mine alone.

At this stage I had fallen into such a wounded place. I had spent so much time and energy trying to mould myself into who I believed was someone that could be accepted and tolerated by another, stemming from this deeply ingrained belief that at the core of my being I was in some way fatally flawed. This is many of our stories, whether or not we are conscious of all the innermost layers of our internal lives. Even this partner, who was the mirror of my wounded self at that time in our lives, was similarly trying hard to fit into a world in which we are all conditioned to be the same.

I look back at myself and feel only compassion for this small self, that I cannot disown if I am to truly integrate and work towards wholeness. I believe that in some way we all have this small self within us, that is deserving of our deepest love and compassion. And when we can find it within ourselves to accept who we were, own all aspects of ourself and our journey without the fear of going backwards, we have the ability to cultivate true compassion and acceptance for others.

We also develop the capacity to see when people around us act from a position founded in the state of their small self. It frees us to shift our own perspective. Instead of getting angry or blaming others for their negative behaviours, we can send them love and compassion when we recognise that they are reacting from an ego driven, wounded place. It empowers us to then make the choice as to how we respond. Do we revert to our own ego driven small-self state and react, or do we act from a place of love, acceptance and grace?

This doesn't mean we allow others to treat us like doormats or walk all over us. It instead means that we learn how to preserve and maintain our own energy and not expend it in conflicts that are unlikely to have a positive outcome. We can only meet people where they are at. My journey as an Empath has taught me that as much as I would like to save everyone from encountering pain and help them reach more joy, contentment, bliss and peace in their lives, it is not my responsibility to do so. Also, it is only ego driven to believe that I have that much power to change any other being except for myself, as I am only responsible for my own emotional state.

Lost, fractured.
Is it only me that feels this way?
Disconnected from the truth?
The truth of WHO I AM.
What do I want?
I don't even know.
Does anyone feel this too?
I think they do.
Where does my truth lie?
Everything from WITHIN. You are bliss. You are truth. You are a part of the sublime manifested into human form.
Don't you see how magnificent you are?
If only you could see how I see you?
Beautiful, truly beautiful soul.

For me after years of trying to fit in and be who I was not, I fell into a very deep depression from which I was uncertain I would ever arise. The thing about depression is, like anything, unless experienced it is such a difficult state for people to truly comprehend. When I talk about depression in this sense, I do not mean days of feeling down or flat, frustrated with a job situation, relationship or life circumstance. I mean the depths of despair, the severe depressive state, the bedridden, lonely, isolatory world, engulfing a person in the deepest of pain, a pain that penetrates to the core of a human soul. These words may sound dramatic, but believe me, those who have entered this state would agree that no amount of expressive words could capture the true essence of how it feels.

For me, the best possible description that fully captures the state of severe depression, is like living in hell here on earth. This is one of the most painful experiences that a human being can encounter. Although usually unhelpful to compare, I think there are some aspects of issues of the mind that add to the suffering. The effect of no one being able to outwardly see the depth of the turmoil within can compound the negative impacts of someone already facing an isolatory internal battle. Also, the outdated beliefs around mental illness as states of weakness or vulnerability, further leave the sufferer alone to fall deeper into the whirlpool of despair.

Living in this state, to put in the context of grief or loss, felt like I was dead but still present here on earth. I have spoken to others who felt similarly. And so, in effect, you experience the grief of the loss of yourself. Imagine grieving your own death. This is a glimpse of the unimaginable, horrifying state that is a severe episode of depression.

After such a long period of heightened anxiety, I am now suffering from depression. This week has probably been the hardest of my life. My core people have been overseas. I felt so desperate that last Friday I started medication. For so many years I had been fearful of it due to the potential side effect of weight gain. I avoided disclosing the extent of my feelings as I knew people would tell me that if I felt that way I needed to try medication. So I was trapped between two mental illnesses intersecting and intertwining to make my life such a struggle and burden to live through.

This week has been like living in isolation. Even though I have seen my dad a few times and two friends, there have been hours and hours of me, alone, just with my painful feelings and irrational thoughts. I have felt like none of them really love me, and that <he> has finally had enough of all of my craziness. I feel like I've become more and more crazy with thoughts of wanting to die and just be over with this emotional turmoil. And the messed up thing that stops me is that if I did anything and it went wrong, then I would end up in hospital, completely out of control. Again trapped between two disorders, one that has become almost protective in a messed up way.

Earlier in the week I thought about <him> coming back and finding me, and how awful it would be for him to find me gone, and feel the burden of guilt that would last a lifetime. But as the feelings grew stronger, the intensity of the pain became so unbearable, that it started to override rational thought. This is the point at which I became fearful, because when your brain is turning against you telling you reasons why your protective factors are not so protective, I could see how people could be pulled to suicide.

Without my core people surrounding me, I have started not being able to feel their love. Rationally I understand they would be devastated if something happened to me, but I just feel so awful inside. It's like this negative beast has taken over me. I feel insane. And so very alone. I have never felt this much pain for such a length of time. When I see the sun, I know rationally that sunlight is joyous and made me feel happy in the past, but I don't feel that joy to my core. I am detached. Numb. My heart is engulfed by darkness, no light is able to penetrate this fog to reach my soul, so burdened within.

I feel so much Pain.
Isolation.
Despair.
Loneliness.
Disgust.
Guilt.
Hatred.
I am unlovable…
Through the darkness into the light…

Things have started to shift for me. The depth of this pain has forced me to be more open and raw with people in my life, resulting in the forging of bonds that never would have occurred. My perspective is starting to shift and my determination to move my life in a new, liberating and freer direction has resurfaced.

By being authentic it has given others the permission to share their own burdens and struggles. And this has surprised me. The commonality of the human spirit shines through, when we are able to discover what is hidden beneath the surface of even the people in our lives we think we know. When we are open with who we are and connect with others in a deeper and truer way, we realise that despite all our differences, we share similarities in our insecurities, our challenges, our fears and our worries.

For me, this period has been a very long time coming. It was building up over many months and years, but as awful and painful as it has been, I do feel stronger, more determined than ever to proceed in the direction of leading a fulfilling and meaningful life. I have no regrets about past decisions and am even grateful for what this experience has taught me about my own strength and capacity to withstand even the most awful of internal experiences. My mind was turning itself against me and I was in such a completely irrational, unclear, foggy state. To think that I felt so desperate that I just wanted to die and cause physical pain to myself to alleviate some of that mental distress and inner pain, seems like a lifetime ago.

A few weeks later…

Time feels like a blur over the past few weeks and months. I have been extremely up and down. <He> is back and the toll this whole thing is taking on both of us is showing. We have also been fighting over the last few days, probably because of the stress we are both under.

I just feel like a yoyo. One moment I'm okay and seemingly feeling better, and the next I'm in the depths of despair, unable to cope with the intensity of my emotions. I never imagined I could be this depressed. I guess once the floodgates were opened everything I have been suppressing for all these years is bursting out.

This is such a cruel illness. Unless people have had a glimpse of it in their own lives, how can anyone begin to comprehend the awfulness and pain it causes, in the heart of the sufferer, who experiences such emotional turmoil and distressing thoughts, and in the hearts of the witnesses, who feel so powerless to help.

A few months later...

The pain is a little bit back today. It's a bit disappointing after a week of good days, but I guess is to be expected, especially with the difficulties between \<him\> and I. What doesn't help is the exacerbation of my ongoing stomach issues, which has been making me feel unwell over the last few days and leaves me feeling so physically and emotionally sick.

I am so very sad. I can see that this depression is completely encompassing my every thought and emotion. I have developed a bit more insight into the fact that it is not me but the depressive cognitions that are engulfing my thinking. When they are so strong though, it is hard not to believe them. I feel like I want someone to just kill me. Put me out of this misery. I am like a diseased dog. Ready to be put down. My whole being is consumed by this depression. It is so cruel. It takes away your connections, your voice, your life. To genuinely experience joy or have moments of pleasure is so fleeting. And simply coping with day-to-day life is like a monumental task. My brain is telling me I can't do it anymore. I know deep within that this is not true and it will pass, but in this moment I am just so desperate, so empty, so lost and above all so sad. If I died it wouldn't be so bad, this would finally be over and I would be gone and soon forgotten. Obliterated from this worldly existence. Just another sad story of someone

Five

Faith

Through all these times I maintained the faith in the inner crevices of my being, that this was not the life I was meant to lead and that incredible things were to come in my life. I always believed even through the most challenging of times, somewhere in the deepest fibres of my being, that I was made of greatness and was to lead an amazing, magical life. And I believe that this is possible for all of us. We are all cut from the same cloth and are all destined for awakening, discovering our true self and connecting with the divine energy of all that is. The challenge is to keep that flame of our inner knowing alive, when faced with these battles that are a part of every human life.

Yet it is a choice we must make. It does not come easily. Every day the universe challenges us in preparation for what it is that we are meant to do in the world. This is the process of shedding all the conditioned belief systems and constructs that have clouded our lives. We need to transcend our small selves, imprisoned by the fears of failure, of being seen and of letting go of people, circumstances or behaviours that no longer serve us, to step into the truth of who we really are.

Slow down.
Stop running. Good things take time.
Patience.
Patience my dear.
You are safe. Breathe.
What is meant for you will never pass you by.
Surrender to the flow of life.
To what is working its way into your consciousness.
Trust that Divine knowing within your heart and soul.
Never doubt what your heart knows.
Trust your heart.
Bypass the chatter.
Mind.
Egoic fear-based patterns.
Cut to the truth.
The essence of who you are.
Who you were always meant to be.
What is your next right move?
Be Here Now.

We are all co-creators with the Universe, and magnificence is up to us to create in our lives. There is no one who leads a life of contentment, fulfilment, happiness and freedom without generating it from within the core of their own being. The journey is one of discovery, as the yogis have identified as a path "to the self, through the self", through the layers of self, to the essence of who we really are.

Yoga and meditation have been practices that have supported me in transcending the limited versions of my smaller self.

How can we make these discoveries, how can we gain any perspective, clarity and wisdom, within the noise of the external world. Now more than ever before in the history of mankind, we are constantly bombarded by a stream of information from the outside world. If we choose to engage with it.

It is essential we find something that gives us the gift of space which may be different for all of us. For some it may be the ocean, for others the bush, but the important thing is to gift ourselves the opportunity to access our inner wisdom.

Yoga and meditation were the practices that allowed me to come into contact with at first small glimpses of silence, space, that then grew as I strengthened my ability to separate from the fluctuations of my mind, emotions, sensations and behaviours. When we start to be able to watch ourselves, what we think, how we feel, how we react to sensations in our body, how we engage with others, we can start to see everything with fresh eyes. Developing this awareness empowers us to slow things down enough to choose our responses.

Will we let our minds drag us down old familiar tracts or will we lay down new pathways in our brain to cultivate gratitude and positivity in our lives? Will we allow emotions to take us over at every opportunity they get, or will we start to cultivate an attitude of acceptance that feelings come and go and nothing lasts forever. We then can allow our feelings to be there with support and compassion for ourselves as we experience them, whilst maintaining the knowledge that they will pass and we will move on to feeling something else.

Pearls of Wisdom:

- Finding avenues where we can access the stillness within is paramount.
- The external world as we know it is fast paced, loud, busy and full of information.
- When we can access a peace within, we are better equipped to hear what our soul is whispering to us.
- We are clearer and more decisive when we tune in to the wisdom of our heart, versus the indecision in our head.

Six

LISTENING TO MY BODY

My interest in yoga and a holistic approach to medicine was very much fuelled by my personal journey and experiences with physical, mental, emotional and spiritual disease. I experienced many years of extremely problematic gut issues, that are known in the medical world as simply IBS (which really is just a cluster of symptoms). Yet my experience of them was anything but simple. At times I would be lying down on the floor due to severe abdominal pain in between consulting patients in GP practice, or when it was at its worst, going for colonic irrigations to relieve the discomfort of chronic constipation.

The impact on my mood and ability to function was one of the greatest challenges of my spiritual journey. I have such a depth of compassion for those suffering from chronic pain and chronic ailments. For me symptoms included severe pain, bloating, reflux and of course the intractable constipation, which many times culminated in a 'spastic colon' meaning it was completely unable to contract and eliminate. From the beginning I knew that the core of the issue was my hypersensitised nervous system, from the external and internal world battles I had been at war with. My body was in a state of constant sympathetic overdrive (the fight or flight mode of activation under stress) and unable to access the parasympathetic rest and digest function that a normal gut can do. It was crying out to me to change many aspects of my internal and external world. Yet for a long time, I would not listen.

I tried every conceivable option which included standard Western medicinal laxatives, increasing fibre, medications and even the colonoscopy preparation which required additional laxatives to work, only to find that my colon was in 'normal' functioning order. I tried acupuncture, yoga, meditation, supplements – including magnesium – potent herbs, the list goes on. Nothing would work. I also saw all different types of practitioners from gastroenterologists to integrative doctors, prescribed antibiotics and laxatives, but found no one understood what I knew was going on in my system.

Of course I believe everything had its role and place along the journey, and led to encounters necessary to facilitate the process of healing. However, it was a challenging and uncomfortable journey to say the least. I tried with all my will and determination to maintain a grateful attitude, which I did, until the fear of this cycle never ending began to consume my being, only further perpetuating the vicious cycle.

Body Wisdom

In my heart I knew I would heal and then be able to use the experience to be of service in the world to others, but the mental challenge of maintaining this belief at times became excruciating.

This beautiful vessel, this beautiful body, it talks to me in every moment, through each and every heart beat.
What is it saying?
What does the language of my spirit say?
Listen, listen.
Stop and hear what only my ears can hear…
Rest, rest if you must, but don't you quit.
Write, read…
But above all keep going.
You are nearly there.
Do medicine on your own unique terms.
Let go of pressures and demands from the outside world and just BE YOU.
There is no other option, otherwise I, your body, will simply slow you down. LISTEN.
I am whispering through the gentleness of the breeze to you…
Will you heed my call?

When I was becoming so despairing that this would never end (at the same holding faith in my heart that it would), I was guided by a friend to a body talk therapist and naturopath. This I felt was the beginning of my true healing. It was the first experience where I found a practitioner who really understood what was happening within my whole system, through the wisdom of communicating with the cells of my body. Through this modality I was able to get in touch with the messages my spirit was crying out for me to hear and heal. This woman maintained such a gentle, compassionate and non-judgemental approach. Through sharing her wisdom she gave me the permission I needed to trust my own intuition and body. She validated everything I had known about the impact of the extreme stress that had caused my body processes to go into shutdown, and helped me learn the tools necessary to heal.

My heart will always be grateful for the sessions we spent together, for her gentle, kind guidance and compassion. It also is an example of the importance of never giving up hope of finding the right person to help you heal. When we are ready, the teacher we need will appear. No sooner or later.

Further along the journey I was gifted to meet another true healer. A beautiful reiki practitioner who mirrored back to me the wisdom I needed to hear from a source outside of myself, to again more deeply trust my intuitive compass and messages from my body. She held the space for me as I finally made peace with the past, found love and compassion for myself in the present and surrendered my future to the universe. It was truly a gift to meet these amazing women. They both embodied my belief in a healer as a guide to connect us more deeply with our body and our higher selves. I will be forever grateful to the universe for granting me the privilege of spending time with such kind-hearted, true, earth angels, acting from a pure place of being of service in the world.

Through my yogic practice and spiritual readings, I also knew this extreme third chakra imbalance was no accident, as the area of the body where disease manifests is no coincidence and is indeed linked to the underlying mental, emotional and spiritual processes related to that part of the body.

Power. Self-esteem. Self-belief. Fire.
For so many years I had struggled with maintaining myself amidst the myriad of perspectives from others around me.
Family.
Partner.
Culture.
I had no sense of my own inner voice or strength.
I felt stuck.

Space…
Where do I end and the other begins?
How do I know what is of me and what is not of me?
Duality, non-duality.
Separation. Unity.
Individual. All one.
We need to exist in our separateness, non-dualistic state to function in our Earth-bound existence, but paradoxically the only way to truly function, to live with presence, awareness, vitality and truth is through our knowledge of our Unity.
Of our interconnectedness.
Of our one divine consciousness.
For without this we are lost.

Empty. Disconnected from who we really are.
Only in our Oneness can we know true Freedom.
Can we truly awaken to the Ecstasy of our Self.
And when we know, we are free.

At one point in desperation to heal these physical issues, I became convinced it was the stress of my job as a GP registrar that was causing me to feel so unwell. I thought that these symptoms were manifesting because I wasn't listening to my soul about my career path. In an effort to follow the truth and not be enslaved by ego demands of the 'right' way to do things, I embarked on a journey into a job in the field of Integrative Medicine.

Through this detour in my career I learnt an invaluable lesson about the path to healing. I saw how any domain of health can become a version of the 'medical model', which didn't resonate for me in the first place. If we place sole emphasis on one thing, be it medications, natural supplements, herbs, acupuncture, yoga, whatever it is, without taking into account the underling thoughts, beliefs, emotional patterns and spiritual dimension, it is unlikely we will be able to heal chronic ailments of the body.

Anything where we are told that the path to health lies in a prescribed way of doing something, is an illusion. There is no one fit for everyone.

The true healers I have encountered know this. They speak differently. They offer up ideas or suggestions, but never prescribed ways of reaching the desired outcome. And so I realised that my way of practising as a healer was better suited to the title of a GP, prompting my return to GP training. Or so I thought.

For 2 years I returned to the path of a GP registrar. I studied for the exams, despite every fibre in my being resisting this direction. The first time I failed and I knew that this wasn't my path. Yet I was not yet strong enough to break away from my conditioning. From the outside voices telling me it was the "golden ticket". So I tried again only to obtain the same result. But this time I knew it was time. Finally I could back my intuitive voice within and question, a golden ticket to what?! To "security"? An illusion anyway. To money? I could never make much anyway, in the way you were expected to see patients in such short time frames. Actually for me it would be a golden ticket to more pain and suffering! And so I finally realised that it was time to embark on my own version of how I believed medicine should be practiced. I would work as a Holistic Doctor and integrate all the knowledge I had obtained from the external world and from within to be of service, follow my call, achieve optimal health and assist others to do the same.

The body holds an innate wisdom that can restore to balance when we get the mind out of the way. Using any modalities, traditional medical or otherwise, are simply tools to support this process.

Something was out of my awareness. What was I missing? I was so confused.
I begged and pleaded with the Universe. What do you want from me?

Leave medicine? I'll do it.
Eat differently. I'll do it.
Separate from my family to develop independence and new belief systems? Fine.
Yet it continued.
Until I finally listened.

I knew that the traditional medical path was not for me.

I have come to make peace with the system of medicine as serving a very important role. Its ability to treat acute presentations, perform surgical intervention and provide a quick solution when our resources to cope with the underlying triggers have been too far stretched, is miraculous in its complexity and skill.

However, when we are faced with chronic issues, things that just keep haunting us or problems that are directly related to the deeper issues in our lives, our mental habits, beliefs, daily behaviours, we need to consider more than the physical domain if we are to truly heal.

I knew I was not the right fit for the quick calls to action or short-term solutions. I was a person of contemplation, reflection and space. And I needed this space! Time with patients, to collaborate, to explore and to guide them back to their own inner voice within.

So I had to step into my truth.
Face my fears.
Financial.
Uncertainty.

Unknown.
Finally I heard.
I had been a fragmented soul. Disconnected and completely VULNERABLE.
Running, running.
Shifted all mental anxiety into the body.
HOLDING ON to all the past FEARS, UNEASE, VIGILANCE.
Finally I have STOPPED.
I feel like I was lost, always floating somewhere above my life but never actually in it, and the more I isolated the more I became sensitised to the outside world.
And now I will heal.
No more running.
No more hyper-vigilance.
I am safe.
I can let people in.
I have a voice now and if someone, anyone, hurts me I can speak up and defend myself.
I reclaim my POWER.
I reclaim my self. My human SELF.
My higher self is here to merge with my lower self.
I am uniting the fragments into WHOLENESS.
Finally. Heard. Need to heal. INTEGRATE.
I am all parts of myself. Past. Now. All one. Fragments slowly coming together.
Painful. Scary.
Emotions. INTENSE.

Who would know?
Own it all.
I am strong and I am vulnerable.
I am powerful and I am afraid.
I am a doctor and I am a yogi.
I am independent and I am interconnected.
I am brave and I am scared.
Courage because of fear.
Masculine. Feminine. Energy.
Faith and trust. I will heal.
This body will return to functioning.
Then I can help others heal.
Gratitude for the journey of learning how to love myself.
Greatest life lesson.
Help others by modelling. Only she who changes herself, changes the world.
"Who looks outside dreams, who looks within awakens."

Pearls of Wisdom:

- Our body is our gateway to our soul.
- Often our mind or ego will dictate its will on our body and when this is out of alignment with our higher self we will manifest illness.
- Symptoms are simply signs that something in our being is out of balance.
- Instead of attempting to rid the body of the symptom, deeper healing comes from raising the question, 'What might the body be trying to say?'

Seven

Body Wisdom

There is a deeper wisdom within our human body that is always trying to communicate to us, in relation to how we are living our lives.

Candace Pert, a professor in the Department of Physiology & Biophysics at Georgetown University School of Medicine, Washington DC, said, "In the end I find I can't separate brain from body. Consciousness isn't just in the head. Nor is it a question of the power of the mind over the body... because they're flip sides of the same thing. Mind doesn't dominate body, it becomes body[1]."

Working in general practice over the last few years, I have seen first-hand the connection between presenting physical complaints and the underlying mental and emotional issues that

---

1 http://www.healingcancer.info/book/export/html/34

drive them. This has been supported in the research by Melbourne GP and senior lecturer at Monash University, Department of General Practice, Craig Hassed, who says, "Over time negative mental and emotional states take a heavy toll on the body and are a significant risk factor for many illnesses[2]."

Our body is constantly trying to send us messages that are more connected with our inner truth. However, often we use our rational thinking minds to override these messages, dictating our will and control on our body, rather than letting our body guide us through life.

In 1964, John Stoeckle and colleagues concluded that 60 to 80 per cent of visits to primary care physicians have a stress-related component[3]. This is a high figure given the predominate view in Western medicine that sees mental and physical health complaints as disconnected; "Our health-care system has been predominantly built on a reactive disease-treatment model rather than a proactive health-enhancement model[4]."

However, there are numerous benefits to facilitating increased patient awareness of the body-mind connection. This approach empowers people to take ownership and self-responsibility for their health, rather than place all their power in the hands of the doctor.

---

[2] Dr Craig Hassed, Mind-Body Medicine: Science, Practice and Philosophy 2007

[3] Stoeckle JD, Zola IK, Davidson GE. The quantity and significance of psychological distress in medical patients: some preliminary observations about the decision to seek medical aid. J Chronic Dis 1964;17:959-970.

[4] A New Era for Mind–Body Medicine. Michelle L. Dossett, M.D., Ph.D., Gregory L. Fricchione, M.D., and Herbert Benson, M.D. April 9, 2020, N Engl J Med 2020; 382:1390-1391

Instead of a 'doctor knows all' approach, we can start to shift the model to a collaborative 'doctor as guide to healing' approach. When I am in clinical practice I often find myself saying to patients that I am simply a source of information, to provide them with all the options to then make the best, most informed decision for them.

I have known many people who have shifted from seeing doctors to seeking alternative modalities, due to feeling disempowered and unhopeful about their health outcomes. What if we could shift the framework to a more empowering and hopeful model, where doctors and patients are working together side by side to facilitate true healing?

Another benefit is the reduction in over-investigation. In our modern world, it is so much easier to order a test, than to support someone by sitting with their fears, when the likelihood of disease identification is low. Risk minimisation at all costs has become our founding principle, due to the fear-based beliefs running our medical system.

Of course appropriate investigation is essential to good clinical practice. This is a given. But managing anxiety and fear through reassurance seeking via investigation is often not the answer. It simply sets up a loop of testing versus self-exploration, when it comes to understanding the connectedness of our integrated human system.

"Symptoms are not enemies to be destroyed, but sacred messengers who encourage us to take better care of ourselves."
Jon Gabriel

With the knowledge about the interconnectedness of our systems, I decided to undertake a small audit into the connection between mind and body, to investigate the impact of the underlying factors at play when patients present with physical issues. I reviewed 100 retrospective presentations and assessed their medical records to determine whether there was any underlying mental or emotional factors precipitating the presenting complaint. Of the presentations, 43 per cent had underlying mental or emotional causes for the presentation.

I then more proactively began to ask my patients, "What is your body trying to tell you?" and conducted a second audit reviewing the data for 100 prospective patients.

Even in cases where we may not expect a connection, like a viral illness or arm pain, this became more overt. Sixty per cent had an underlying mental or emotional cause for the presentation. An increase of 17 per cent.

What this reflects is the deeper wisdom of our bodies. As doctors the time has come for us to embark on a new system of health care, where we guide patients to hear the messages their bodies are trying to communicate with them.

This brief audit made me reflect on prior patients I had seen in GP. For example, I recalled a woman who initially presented with fatigue and stress. She was always putting herself last and overworking. It took months before she listened to her body and was then diagnosed with papillary thyroid cancer. However, once the anxiety over the diagnosis subsided, the thyroid was removed and she gave herself the time to heal. In this process she realised how imbalanced her priorities had been. The whole experience prompted her to spend more time with her family, work less and start the journey of taking care of herself as part of her lifestyle.

As doctors we need to question whether we want to be governed by principles of an old model of health-care provision and healing that are no longer serving us or our patients, or if is it time to step into something new. The number of doctors becoming burdened by their own mental health issues is on the rise.

The results of a survey published by Beyond Blue in October 2013 showed that the rates of depression in more than 14,000 doctors and medical students were over four times higher than in the general population[5]. I believe the impact of a system in which the patient has been conditioned to place all responsibility for their health onto the doctor, is one of the contributing factors to these figures. We cannot carry the pain and suffering of everyone we meet.

It is time for a new era of medicine. Each one of us carries our answers from a wisdom within. It is now time for the doctor to become the guide to healing. Life is not just about being free of illness or disease, but of shifting to a state of optimal health, wellness, contentment and joy.

---

[5] *Beyond Blue (2013). National Mental Health Survey of Doctors and Medical Students – Executive summary. http://www.beyondblue.org.au/media/media-releases/media-releases/action-to-improve-the-mental-health-of-australian-doctors-and-medical-students*

The period of time prior to my consultation with Dr Talia I had been unwell, with varied symptoms, ear infections, throat infection, constantly tired and finally my body presented me with shingles.

I presented to Dr Talia who listened to my story and noted my previous health conditions. Dr Talia asked me, "What do you think your body is saying to you?" I was quite surprised, as this is not a question regularly asked by doctor to patient. Dr Talia asked again, "What do you think your body is saying to you?" As this question was posed to me numerous times, I had to take a moment to contemplate the answer. I then replied, "I think my body is telling me to stop and slow down."

After the initial realisation I felt very emotional. Yes, my body was talking to me and telling me to slow down. Dr Talia then asked, "What can you do to listen to your body?" I was able to take time off work and allow my body to repair itself in the state of rest.

I do believe that I could have continued in a spiral of poor health if Dr Talia had not asked the question, and empowered me to listen to my body.

In retrospect it is the principles of a holistic health model that gave me the time to gain personal insights into my life – including personal interactions, the career I was pursuing, the workplace – that had all contributed to my general poor health. Since making the decision to leave the workplace and take time to nurture myself, my health has recovered. I feel so much better prepared to approach life with clarity of that which is important, being aware of what can influence and build one's spirit and protect the body.

Thank you Dr Talia for your time and courage to work in a holistic health model.

59 yo female patient

Pearls of Wisdom:

- A healer is a guide to assist us in connecting more deeply with ourself.
- All our answers are within, however we are human beings and we all need guides and mentors to help us along the way.

Eight

How to Listen to our Body

I have found that due to the busyness of life in our modern world, amidst so much external and internal noise, it can be very hard for people to even know where to start when it comes to tuning into the messages of their body.

This is where the power of meditation can assist us.

Meditation can give us this space to connect inwards, listen and then really hear what internal messages our body is trying to deliver.

I have also found the written word to be a very powerful tool.

If we combine meditation with expressive journalling, we can take both practices even deeper to allow the answers we have been searching for to arise from within us.

My invitation to you is to connect with this inner wisdom of your body, to uncover the hidden messages that are waiting to be heard.

All you need is a quiet space, a pen and paper, to stop, disconnect from the noise of the world and tune in to the wisdom within.

Meditation Exercise

Sit or lie down in a comfortable position.

Gently still your body, closing down the eyes.

Take a deep breath in and exhale everything out.

Start to bring your awareness to your feet. Your precious feet that carry you wherever you go. See if you can bring a sense of gratitude to this often neglected part of your body. Taking a big breath in then sigh everything out.

Then gently bring your awareness up your calves to your knees and then your thighs. Notice any tension or tightness in your legs and see if you can allow it to gently soften. Taking a big breath in and then sighing everything out, letting it all go.

Start to become aware of where your body meets the chair or the earth beneath you, tuning in to each point of connection. Notice any sensations around your hips, your buttocks, just noticing.

Allow your awareness to rest on your hands. Notice any sensations, any tingling or movement of energy. Your hands are the loving extension of your heart. Bring a sense of gratefulness to these parts of your body that enable you to do so much.

Gently allow your awareness to move up to your heart space. Notice any sensations here. Notice the feeling of your heart beating in your chest, or the gentle movement of air into your body. Just noticing.

Then allow your awareness to shift to your neck and shoulders. Often this is an area of our bodies where we store a lot of tension. Notice what you find here. Gently shrug your shoulders on the inhale and then as you exhale let everything go.

Then gently bring your awareness to your face. Notice any tension or tightness around your eyes, temples or jaw. See if you can allow it to soften. Take a big breath in and exhale everything out, letting go any stresses or thoughts that are no longer serving you.

Finally, bring your awareness to your belly, noticing the rise and fall with each breath. As you breathe in allow the belly to gently rise and as you breathe out letting everything go. Let your breath fill every cell of your body with a sense of energy and aliveness. Connecting with your entire body as one.

From this calm and centred space start to contemplate the question, "What is your body trying to tell you?"

Without judgement, notice the first thing that comes to your conscious mind.

Take another deep breath in and exhale everything out, tuning in to the inner wisdom of your body.

What is your body trying to tell you?

Take another deep breath in and exhale.

What is your body trying to tell you?
Take another deep breath in and exhale.
What is your body trying to tell you?
Take another deep breath in and exhale.
What is your body trying to tell you?
When you are ready, you can gently open your eyes.

You might like to take some time to write down any messages you may have uncovered from tuning in to your body's inner wisdom, without trying or thinking, rather letting the messages from within flow onto the page.

Now you have heard.

The choice is yours to make.

The only question is, will you listen?

Pearls of Wisdom:

- Trust the messages that you hear from within.
- And even if you hear nothing, that itself is something. It is a sign that you may like to start the journey of learning how to connect with your body.
- Investing time and energy are necessary to developing a good relationship with oneself. And this is valuable as it is the most important relationship you will ever have.

Nine

The Path to Healing

Moving from the wounded position of an ego dominated mind to a freer state of wellness, is not something I believe that anyone can offer a formula or method to reach.

It is an illusory idea to believe that anyone can offer us a direct route to our own healing.

The only truth I have discovered thus far on my journey is that the most important factor in finding inner health, wellbeing, peace, freedom and contentment, is learning to tune in to the wisdom within.

The more we learn to practise authenticity in thought, word and action, the more we learn to act in ways which serve our inner being. It is only by tuning in that we can be guided along our own unique path to healing.

Body Wisdom

The modalities themselves don't matter. The diet itself doesn't matter. The exercise regime, the supplements, the type of therapy or energy work we engage in, doesn't matter.

Ultimately what matters is learning how to forge a path in this life that is our own. Our bodies are trying to wake us up to this.

They are guiding us to our inner truths. To listen to the voice of our highest self.

To live a rich and full life, filled with adventure and experiences that make us feel alive.

Life is meant to be joyous and happy, and when we give ourselves permission to live in this way, anything is possible.

I have learnt that it is a virtue to maintain an open mind, but with this we must maintain discernment. We must decide what resonates for us on our path to health. No practitioner knows our own body as well as we do. Each person we meet is a guide, with lessons or knowledge to share with us if it fits what we need.

The path to healing is the path to self-understanding.

They are one and the same.

There is a reason for everything we experience.

Trust the unfolding and allow the wisdom of your body to be your guiding compass to the life that you desire.

Pearls of Wisdom:

- Anything is a tool.
- There is no straight line, one-fix solution to healing.
- Ultimately, finding what resonates with oneself is the key to facilitating any significant change.

Ten

Messages from within our own body

What my eyes have seen, what my heart has borne witness to within, has no comparison to anything that could happen without.

Whatever external circumstances we are faced with, we always have the ability to turn within, to the sanctuary within our very own mind, if we choose to create it.

It can be a wonderful heaven or a tumultuous hell.

The choice is ours.

What will you choose?

Love, peace, freedom, ease or fear, unease, dissatisfaction?

What is in one is in the whole.

No matter what external circumstances we face, the internal feeling states are the same.

Let go conditioning.

Pain is inevitable. It is part of human life.
But suffering, suffering is optional.

The human mind is one of the most complex instruments there is. Each human being contains a world within, a world that others are only offered glimpses into when we truly connect and feel safe with another. My intention for sharing my story is to illustrate what happens when we go against the messages our body is trying to communicate to us. To show how when we go against the natural flow and order of things we create our very own suffering. However, when we stop and listen, we each contain an inner wisdom that can serve to direct us in the transformation of our lives.

It is like the contrast of two wolves in our mind as the old parable goes…

An old Cherokee is teaching his grandson about life, 'A fight is going on inside me,' he said to the boy. 'It is a terrible fight, and it is between two wolves. One represents anger, envy, sorrow, regret, greed, arrogance, self-pity, guilt, resentment, inferiority, lies, false pride, superiority and ego.' He continued, 'The other one represents joy, peace, love, hope, serenity, humility, kindness, benevolence, empathy, generosity, truth, compassion and faith. The same fight is going on inside of you and inside of every person, too.' The grandson thought about it for a minute and then asked his grandfather: 'Which wolf will win?' The old Cherokee simply replied, 'The one you feed.'

My journey has propelled me to explore the depths of my mind, from delving into the darkest of places to elevating into sublime, ecstatic states, learning slowly the ability to bring these extremes into balance and working towards a more constant state of equanimity. I have wanted to share the darkness that can so often go glossed over, not for the intent of feeding this shadow 'wolf' side, but to give hope to those currently facing this part of themselves that there is always the capacity to shift into the lightness and connect with the truth of your being. Which is pure love.

Yet the integration of self is a journey of a lifetime, or lifetimes.

Also, my intention is to illuminate the human condition of struggle to enlightenment as a universal experience. We all have challenges, we all have obstacles to overcome, and identifying our own set of difficulties as more challenging than another's is simply an over-active ego at work. And why is this even useful to contemplate?

The importance of this concept is that it is up to each of us to say to ourselves, "I accept where I am, I accept the difficulties I may be encountering today and have encountered in the past, but this is not where my journey is going to end." We need to be brave, courageous and strong to tackle the darkness within, endure the pain of change and acknowledge our truths in the hope and faith that by doing so we will enable our soul to make peace with itself, empowered to live a more content and authentic existence.

Each one of us has the power within to achieve this, as the answers are not to be found in the external world, but instead from listening to the messages from within our own body.

Pearls of Wisdom:

- Ultimately, we have two paths in our mind.
- It is our choice which one we will follow.
- Yet we are all human and are all on the same path.
- We will choose darkness at some point whether on a small or large scale.
- However, in every moment we have the capability to choose again and transmute suffering into the light.
- Life can be the joyous, miraculous adventure that we so desire.

About the Author

Dr Talia Steed MBBS

Dr Talia completed her Bachelor of Medicine at the University of Western Australia in 2009.

Following this she embarked on her internship year at Fremantle Hospital. In 2011 she commenced training in the field of psychiatry. However after three years she took time off to take care of her mental health and begin her own healing journey.

Due to her persistent curiosity in the workings of the human mind and desire to help others, Dr Talia went on to complete a Certificate in Counselling at Murdoch University. She also trained in Gestalt psychotherapy for two years and attended workshops in Acceptance and Commitment Therapy.

Subsequently she went on to work in the field of general practice, whilst at the same time obtaining her yoga teacher qualification over a two-year program in Perth.

However what Dr Talia found, was that the way she wanted to practice medicine was with a whole body, mind and spirit approach. This led her to her unique Holistic Health model in which she integrates her allopathic medical training with her spiritual foundation as a Holistic Doctor.

Acknowledgments

This book has taken its own lifetime of evolution into fruition, with excerpts from some of my writing from over 10 years ago.

It would certainly not have manifested into the physical form without the support and guidance of my mentor Iggy Tan.

He saw something in my story.

I am so grateful to Iggy for his kindness, his inspiration, his dedication and humility.

The evolution of this book, corresponded with my own evolution, and I am so grateful to those along the way, who supported, and inspired my path.

Special mention to Katherine Stinson, Naturopath and Body Talk practitioner, Elaine Macleod, Reiki practitioner and Odette Linton, Body Talk practitioner and Spiritual Healer, women of the highest integrity, spirit and strength. These women showed me to trust in myself. To let go the limitations of the outside world. And to know, that we are always being supported and guided by the Universe.

Final Dedication

To my dear Stephen.
The love we share is a Miracle.
You bring me the greatest joy beyond what
I could ever have imagined.
I cherish every moment we spend together.
You inspire me.
You support me.
You energise and enliven me.
My life is even more blessed to have you in it.
I am forever grateful to the Universe for bringing us together.

www.ingramcontent.com/pod-product-compliance
Lightning Source LLC
Chambersburg PA
CBHW050320010526
44107CB00055B/2331